NAME YOUR EMOTIONS

SOMETIMES I FEEL ANGRY

by Jaclyn Jaycox

PEBBLE
a capstone imprint

Pebble Emerge is published by Pebble, an imprint of Capstone.
1710 Roe Crest Drive
North Mankato, Minnesota 56003
www.capstonepub.com

Library of Congress Cataloging-in-Publication Data is available on the
Library of Congress website.
ISBN 978-1-9771-2464-7 (library binding)
ISBN 978-1-9771-2640-5 (paperback)
ISBN 978-1-9771-2507-1 (eBook PDF)

Summary: What does it mean to be angry? Anger may not make us
feel good, but it's an emotion everybody has! Children will learn how
to identify when they are angry and ways to manage their feelings.
Large, vivid photos help illustrate what anger looks like. A mindfulness
activity will give kids an opportunity to explore their feelings.

Image Credits
Capstone Studio: Karon Dubke, 21; Shutterstock: Africa Studio,
19, Anastasiia Markus, 18, Annashou, 5, Color Symphony, Design
Element, Dmytro Zinkevych, 15, fizkes, 17, Kira Garmashova, 13,
pixelheadphoto digitalskillet, 11, RanQuick, 9, Syda Productions, Cover,
wavebreakmedia, 6, WIRACHAIPHOTO, 7, Zdan Ivan, 12

Editorial Credits
Designer: Kay Fraser; Media Researcher: Tracy Cummins; Production
Specialist: Katy LaVigne

Printed and bound in China.
3322

TABLE OF CONTENTS

Words in **bold** are in the glossary.

WHAT IS ANGER?

Have you ever fought with a friend? Have your parents told you to clean your room, but you didn't want to? These things may have made you feel angry.

Anger is an **emotion**, or feeling. People have lots of different feelings every day. Being angry can make us feel bad. But it is OK to feel angry sometimes.

WHAT DOES IT FEEL LIKE TO BE ANGRY?

Think of a time when you were angry. Maybe someone was calling you names. Or you got **blamed** for something you didn't do. How did you feel?

When you are angry, you start breathing faster. Your face gets red. You feel like you want to scream and yell. You might feel like stomping your feet.

USING YOUR SENSES

Everyone has five **senses**. People can touch, taste, hear, see, and smell things. Your senses send messages to your brain. That's where feelings start.

Hearing someone laugh at you can make you feel angry. Seeing rain when you want to play outside might make you angry.

9

TALKING ABOUT YOUR FEELINGS

Talking about your feelings is important. It's not good to keep angry feelings inside. If you are angry, tell someone you care about. Explain why you feel this way. It can help you calm down. It helps others find ways to make you feel better too.

UNDERSTANDING ANGER

Everyone gets angry at times. Anger is caused by different things. Sometimes you are angry at others. If your brother breaks your favorite toy, you might get angry.

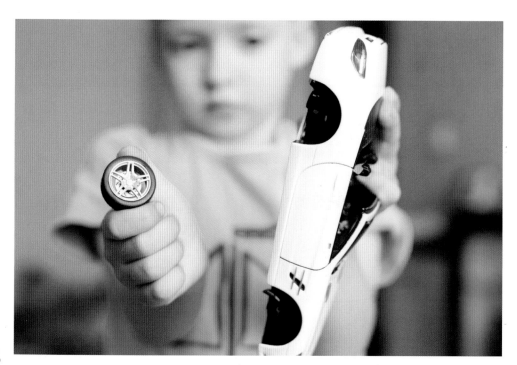

Other times, you may be angry at
yourself. If you are having a hard time
with your homework, you might feel angry.

Anger can be a helpful emotion. It can make you feel **brave**. If someone is teasing you, you may feel brave enough to stand up for yourself.

Anger can also spark change. Seeing someone throw trash on the ground might make you angry. You could ask your family to spend time cleaning up trash outside.

HANDLING YOUR FEELINGS

Anger can be a strong feeling. It's important to know how to deal with it. You don't want your anger to get too big. No one should ever hurt someone out of anger.

There are things you can do to calm down. You can take a deep breath. Then count to 10. Your bad feelings will start to go away.

You can give someone a hug. Try thinking good thoughts. Turn on some happy music and dance. Run around outside.

You can help others who are angry too.
Give them space to calm down. Think of
ways you could help them feel happy.
Let them know you are there for them.

MINDFULNESS ACTIVITY

Sometimes emotions get really big. Try this to see what emotions might look like in your head.

What You Do:

1. Put about ½ inch (1.3 centimeters) of glitter in the bottom of a clear jar.

2. Add warm water until the jar is almost full.

3. Put in 2 or 3 drops of dish soap.

4. Screw the lid on tightly and shake, shake, shake!

Just like the glitter, your emotions can swirl around in your head before finally calming down.

GLOSSARY

blame (BLAME)—to hold yourself or someone else responsible for something that happened

brave (BRAVE)—showing strength and willingness to do difficult things

emotion (i-MOH-shuhn)—a strong feeling; people have and show emotions such as happiness, sadness, fear, anger, and jealousy

sense (SENSS)—a way of knowing about your surroundings; hearing, smelling, touching, tasting, and sight are the five senses

READ MORE

Hasson, Gill. *Take Charge of Anger*. Minneapolis: Free Spirit Publishing, 2019.

Kreul, Holde. *My Feelings and Me*. New York: Skyhorse Publishing, 2018.

INTERNET SITES

Kids' Health – Taking Charge of Anger
kidshealth.org/en/kids/anger.html

PBS Kids – Draw Your Feelings
pbskids.org/arthur/health/resilience/draw-your-feelings.html

INDEX